The Small Book of Big Marketing
The Foundations of the Markenomics System in the Palm of Your Hand.

The Small Book of Big Marketing

All rights reserved. No part of this book can be reproduced, in whole or part, in any form, or by electronic or mechanical means, without the prior consent of the author.

Copyright (c) 2015 by Ned Fasullo
Cover Design by Ned Fasullo
Self Published through Blurb Books

To order additional copies of the book or for further information on Ned Fasullo, visit www.sbobm.com, and in most online bookstores.

This book is dedicated to:

- All of my friends, colleagues and acquaintances in the profession of Marketing. You all know who you are and remember – never stop innovating, being relevant and thinking different.
- Mary Joy Fasullo, my oldest daughter who inspires me every day to write, write, write. You have the biggest heart of anyone I know and I look forward to watching you grow into a great writer.
- Lucy Fasullo, my youngest daughter, who inspires me every day to think young, think fun, have a big smile and always, always be ready to pick a flower when we see it. Just because we can.

Disclaimer: The concepts, views and opinions expressed in this book are solely attributed to the author unless otherwise noted. The purpose of this book is to provide a foundation and starting point for those interested in applying these concepts into their Marketing strategy.

About the author: Ned Fasullo is a 22 year veteran of sales & marketing technology, internet technologies, advertising media, an advanced technologist, entrepreneur, business owner, public speaker, polymath, current Chief Marketing Officer and creator of "Markenomics: Connection, Engagement, Conversion and the Evolution of the Practice" Training System.

"I hope that you enjoy this book. It was tough to write. I really don't know how professional writers do it because dragging this information out of my head was exhausting to say the least. It's meant to be a primer to bigger and better things and I hope that it brought some measure of interest and made you stop and think.

If you or your company is interested in my Markenomics Training(c) System, please don't hesitate to contact me for more information and please feel free to follow me on Social Media channels. Thanks for reading!"

Ned Fasullo

Table of Contents:

Page 6	The Markenomics Equation
Page 15	Messaging the Core Values
Page 19	Content Types
Page 25	Content Personas
Page 32	Content Channels
Page 37	Your Marketing Team
Page 44	Target Company Profile
Page 49	Lead Generation & Lead Scoring
Page 55	Marketing Intelligence
Page 61	K.A.R.E. Customers
Page 66	Product Development
Page 74	Sales Enablement
Page 78	Marketing & Data Science
Page 87	Why Marketing Matters
Page 94	The 12 Impact Points of Marketing
Page 103	Glossary of Marketing Acronyms
Page 119	Professional Organizations & Associations
Page 122	Professional Certifications
Page 127	Events & Conferences
Page 134	Marketing Technology Landscape
Page 136	In Closing

"Markenomics in its purest form is the coordinated execution of analytics, intelligence, strategy and service, to produce a desired, and repeatable, economic result."

Ned Fasullo

The Markenomics Equation(c)

So here's how it started. I realized early on in my career in sales that the most successful people and sales organizations managed themselves through CRM (customer relationship management) platforms. And by early I mean 1997(ish). One of the things that really stood out about the company I worked for a the time was that they had taken the initiative to not only utilize CRM in their organization, but that they had created their own platform and had built all of the customization around how they needed to do business each day. Being that they were in the business of software development and web, this came easy to them. I can remember going to present our software platforms to very large clients at the time, most of them who had their own sales organizations, and logging in to the CRM to launch the demo. Generally, about nine out of ten times, after the demo was over, they would ask us to show them "that other system" we had logged in to and to tell them more about that one. What I soon began to realize was that in the mid-to-late 90's the most valuable platform a business with a sales organization could leverage, besides their financial systems, was a CRM platform.

The CRM allowed them to measure and manage their clients and prospects unlike anything before it, but it also seeded the ideas for what we are seeing today in the discipline of Marketing – Big Data. Little did we know all those years ago, but we were directly responsible for the foundations of what almost two decades of dependence on CRM's has resulted in the Big Data boom, but I digress....

Fast forward to today, and I am the new CMO for a much larger company. I come in the first few months looking through CRM data to start to understand what we have going for us. I find immediately that the company, which at the time is in the beginning phases of a major market transition, doesn't fully know what their data is all about. And by that I mean, don't have a clear picture of almost any of it. This is not to say the company was failing in how it operated, in fact quite the contrary.

They had grown very rapidly during the preceding decade and as I dug deeper I started to see that about every 48 months their growth had caused them to out pace their internal systems. So the CRM was "there" but it was not in any shape to provide meaningful data of much use. What was important though was that the company was beginning a massive transition from predominantly product-based sales to a mix of products with a lot of recurring services business. The need for clean CRM data and a much more structured approach to the use of CRM had just become a top priority for me, if I hoped at all to be successful in this role.

After roughly 4 months of rallying other management behind the cause of cleaning up the CRM, I was able to begin showing the fruits of the labor by providing some very elementary reporting on the CRM data. A year later, we were able to marry that data to the financial records to start to show a 3-4 year run on the customers financial life-cycle with us. But we were still missing quite a bit. I knew that in order to continue growing in a positive direction, we had to take this data to the next level and begin looking at marketing automation and a new CRM platform. More on that later.

Around spring of 2014 in the middle of these issues, I had an epiphany. There should be a way to express the concept of data-driven marketing with a simple formula that would be instantly understandable to most marketing professionals, and be accepted by his or her peers in management, or in the case of the CMO, be able to mingle with the rest of the C-suite.

Lets breakdown the formula into its basic parts. Again I don't see this as some genius answer to a mythical problem, but it allowed me to also visualize in a much different way, the way to solve the problem that I now faced – how to extract the value from the data and quantify the necessary steps across the business that we needed to achieve the success we were looking for.

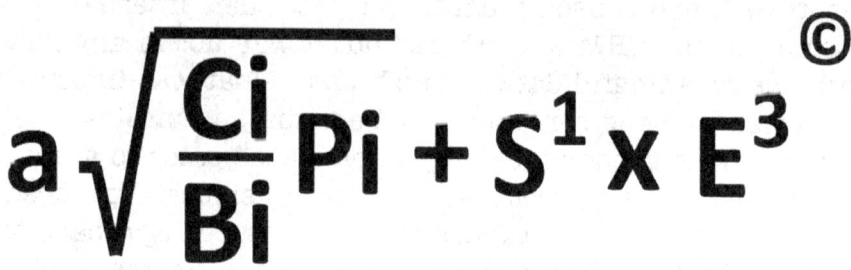

$$a\sqrt{\frac{Ci}{Bi}}Pi + S^1 \times E^3 \;\copyright$$

a=Analytics. Big Data is the water in the bucket. Once your bucket is full, you can then decide the best ways to use the water in different places. Maybe its in the flower bed, refilling the dog's bowl, or washing the car. The key is that until the water is in the bucket, you can't do squat. The analytics piece is the catalyst for the formula. It starts everything.

Bi=Business Intelligence. The Bi variable is where the data gets interesting. This is where you have the data at a point where it can be easily viewed, manipulated and shared in a way that can begin to answer questions. Questions like "who are our best customers?", "what is their average spend?", "what verticals are we more heavy in?", etc. The BI is the way that we begin to quantify the data into subsets and report on it so that we can act.

Ci=Competitive Intelligence. The Ci variable brings you a wealth of information on what your nearest competitors are doing (good and bad). There are many ways to collect this data both officially and unofficially and it allows the organization to address the difference in how the customers perceive you, buy in, purchase and repeat.

Pi=Product Intelligence. The Pi variable provides you with data directly from the marketplace. This helps you to define from a focused perspective, what products are in the market, their value proposition, their position of market-share, and their differentiation to you. When researching product intelligence, try and approach it agnostically from the point of being a customer. This allows you to see the offerings a little more holistically and really gain insight to what is in front of you.

S=Strategy (go-to-market). Once you have your core analytics, your business intelligence, competitive intelligence and product intelligence, you have the foundation for defining your value proposition in the marketplace. It also gives you the hyper focused approach needed for training, development, sales and support of your offerings. Strategy is determined by as few people as possible to accelerate design, deployment and control. Essentially, this is the role that Marketing needs to be driving.

E=Execution. Most believe that this variable is only for the sales teams. This could not be more untrue. Execution has three components in the Marketing Formula. The first component is most obviously, marketing. Marketing must execute across all its lines and provide detailed metrics on where the majority of the responses are coming from, lead scoring, etc. Second is the sales aspect. Sales must take the information from Marketing and meet with customers to close business. Once business is closed, the third aspect comes in and that is support. After the deals are in house, the operations teams must provide legendary support and assistance to begin the first steps of the customer's life-cycle with the organization, and maintain these levels to assure that marketing can re-communicate and sales can continue to attach more business to the customer account. Execution is the responsibility of the entire organization because at the end of the day it's a team effort.

Essentially I looked at the overall information that I needed on hand to create my knowledge base, from which we develop go-to-market strategy, execute and then measure. This formula is purposely built around execution to grow revenue.

If done correctly I admit that it can offer ancillary benefits such as mind-share, strengthening of the brand, etc., but my goal as I view marketing in a B2B environment is to be a catalyst and influencer of revenue growth. I have a hard time justifying the marketing spend of time and/or money to develop a brand, because a B2B customer is not the same as a B2C consumer. But that's a subject for another book.

Is the Formula Immutable?

The real answer here is **no**. This formula is a starting point for almost any business to begin its quest. The goal is for every business to get started and over time make adjustments to the formula to take into account specific areas of your operations that are different from others.

A great formula is only as good as the variables used to build it. As with most business formulas, the variables can and will be different depending on the action and the outcome you are attempting to measure.

I encourage the reader to take this formula as a starting point. If it works as is, then that's okay too, but a starting point you now have! Use it as it is. Put the principals into play to start to get a better understanding of what this brings to the organization, how it affects what you do and how you do it when going to market with your products and services. From there, the skies the limit.

NOTES:

"I think that if you picked any company as a template and pretended that company was the government of the United States, Marketing would be a combination of the CIA and Department of Tourism. Our main job is to have you come in and feel warm and cozy. The other part of the job is building scenarios from data sets, gathering as much product, business and competitive intelligence as possible, and then instructing leadership and/or senior management based on the relevant data."

Ned Fasullo

Messaging the Core Values

In order to perform properly as a marketer, it cannot be stressed enough that the professional marketer *must have a very clear and very deep understanding of the organization they work for*. The Marketer must know at a minimum:

The Organization's Core Values. Or mission statement or whatever the organization you work for calls it. Core Values can differentiate one company from another any day of the week.

What's the Passion. Why do people work for your organization? What is the passion that drives them to show up everyday and support your customers?

What is the Organization 'Best At'? Put simply, what does your organization 'kick ass' at? What is your nomdeplume, or claim to fame?

What are the Economic Drivers that Draw Customers Attention? When you sell your product/service to your customers, what are the economic drivers associated with your solutions that help to convince your customers that doing business with you is a win-win?

This chapter will be focused on messaging the Core Values. Content design must account for some level of visibility and constant reminder of the organization's Core Values.

The reason they are so vital to content marketing is that they specify what kinds of content you should create, and more importantly, what kinds of content you cannot create.

Having your core values be compact, easy to understand, and meaningful gives "guard rails" for your content marketing strategy.

Zappos states their values as:

1. *Deliver WOW Through Service*
2. *Embrace and Drive Change*
3. *Create Fun and A Little Weirdness*
4. *Be Adventurous, Creative, and Open-Minded*
5. *Pursue Growth and Learning*
6. *Build Open and Honest Relationships With Communication*
7. *Build a Positive Team and Family Spirit*
8. *Do More With Less*
9. *Be Passionate and Determined*
10. *Be Humble*

If you're working on an info-graphic at Zappos and you've got some data that contradicts a main point, the value of Open and Honest Relationships With Communication should override the expedient tactic of simply ignoring something you don't agree with.

Ask yourself this: how often do you consult your core values when you're creating content? The more you can integrate them into your work-flow and creation process, the more likely you will create content that has a consistent voice and point of view. You'll also be less likely to create PR and marketing disasters that deeply offend people if you're constantly checking to make sure your content is aligned with your values.

NOTES:

"Marketing is a proactive action. Content is a message. Advertising is a medium for distribution of the message. Customer Service is a timely, successful response. Brand is a successful outcome of all of this."

Ned Fasullo

Content Types

Marketing today is all about CONTENT. If Big Data is the engine, content is the gasoline that makes the engine run at optimal performance. Everything you will do (or should do) in a Markenomics environment is based in content. Creating content on different scales for use in different channels to achieve your call-to-action and/or goals is paramount. What content works? That's a tough question to simply make a blanket statement to because businesses are all different. That said, here are some of the most relevant and common types of content that are making waves and bringing the action.

--> *Subject matter articles*
--> *Product driven articles*
--> *Press announcements*
--> *New hire announcements*
--> *Awards & certifications announcements*
--> *Customer Testimonials*
--> *White papers & Tech specs*
--> *User & Training manuals*
--> *and more...*

While this is by no means the only types, these are some of the most relevant types that you are seeing on business websites that include an email sign up and a call-to-action of some kind. What's more important to note is that content consumption on mobile is growing exponentially and many marketers are not creating content based on 'responsive design'. Responsive design is a practice where the content is delivered to the end user through any channel and its look and feel adapt to the needs of the display device. So one piece of content would display agnostically across multiple screens for the end user. Not instituting a policy of responsive design means that your content creation must be altered for each possible display device out there, i.e. ALL mobile handsets, PC & laptop screens, etc.

8 Types of Content You Must Incorporate into Your Strategy.

Content marketing gets a lot of buzz these days, and for good reason. It only costs time to create, it sticks around forever, it helps your search engine rankings, it improves your visibility, it reinforces your brand, and it encourages people to buy from you -- all in one package.

That being said, certain types of content work and certain types do not. Be sure you're using these eight types of content in your strategy:

1) Opinion pieces. Even if it's controversial, state your opinion boldly. You'll get attention and encourage discussion no matter what.

2) Company accomplishments and directives. Press releases are perfect for capturing these, but you can also run with them in blog posts.

3) Instructions and guides. "How-to" articles are incredibly popular, especially if you include step-by-step instructions with pictures and videos.

4) Statistics and trends. Infographics are the best content medium for these, but you can also analyze them in a blog. Be sure to reference all facts appropriately.

5) Product spotlights. If you have a new product featured, or are using something new in your business -- write about it! Be as objective and informative as possible, and don't make it a sales piece.

6) Business interviews. Interview someone within your company or someone big in the industry.

7) Specific advice. If your customers or your audience have common problems, write an advice-style column to address it.

8) Questions and answers. Short Q&A features are very popular, and are great for optimizing your website for long-tail keywords in the form of questions.

And as a bonus, here are a few types of content you should not use as part of your content marketing strategy:

- **Pushy or blatant sales content.** Your blog shouldn't be home to digital sales flyers. Your goal is to be an authority, not a billboard.

- **Copied or plagiarized content.** Never copy and paste unless you're quoting someone, and if you're expanding on someone else's content, be sure to put your own spin on it.

- **Keyword-stuffed content.** SEO is alive and well, but if you pack keywords into your blogs for the sole purpose of gaining ranks, you'll be fishing for a Google penalty and alienating your readers.

It will take some time to find your voice and perfect your strategy, but once you do, you'll be reaping the benefits of your hard work in no time.

NOTES:

"I believe that their use of marketing and pop-culture icons as a strategic play to enhance their brand cements the innovation of their products and creates an energy that causes normal people to want to be extraordinary just by using their stuff." (on Apple)

Ned Fasullo

Content Personas

Understanding the heirarchy of the organization is critical. All of the C-level executives, VP's, and upper level management are stake-holders. Middle management are the executors, and regular employees are the trench warfare folks. The C-level executives, VP's and upper level management are those that relevant content means everything to. Understanding their role in the organization, their challenges, and building a relationship around helping them achieve their goals is the key.

Each member of a buying team has different challenges and interests. You must build content that is relevant to the target client persona. Stop emailing the IT director, and start bringing relevant business information and articles about the problems facing the client/client vertical, to the decision makers in those areas. For example, all healthcare organizations are facing issues around data and communications compliance. Who is in charge of those outcomes in the organizations? That is the Target Client Persona that you will seek to influence with the highly specialized content surrounding data and communications compliance. Not the IT manager but the person who's job depends on this area being successful.

Personas should include a full portrait of your ideal buyer — including information like:

Demographic/background information:
--> Job title, career, roles and responsibilities
--> Family/life outside work, household income
--> Company size, location and industry
--> Budget

Behavioral information:
--> What keeps them up at night
--> Pain points and challenges
--> Role in purchasing
--> Content consumption

Here's an example:

VP of Marketing – Interested in understanding how the agency can fulfill his or her company's needs (higher search engine rankings, content creation and promotion, paid search) and examples of success. Typically the overall decision maker.

Relevant content includes: Web copy (explaining products/services) case studies, interviews with customers and thought-leadership pieces.

CFO/Controller – Mainly concerned with the pricing model (retainer or service-based payments?), total investment and potential ROI. Usually has a definitive role in the decision-making process.

Relevant content includes: price sheets and case studies with ROI metrics.

In addition to creating content that relates to each buyer persona's pain points, your content should also map back to a stage in the buyer's journey. Though buyers will fluctuate between stages — the buying cycle is often nonlinear — the following are generally the three stages each buyer goes through before making a purchase decision:

Awareness: The buyer knows he or she has a problem that needs to be solved and searches for content that confirms that need and your business' ability to fix it. Awareness-stage content also typically includes thought-leadership and third-party content that aligns a brand's message with experts in the industry, though is often vendor neutral.

Consideration: In the consideration stage, the buyer is researching solutions and is looking for content that speaks directly to specific pain points. In this stage, buyer personas are essential, as each persona experiences different challenges that must be addressed through vendor-published content.

Decision: At this stage, the buyer is ready to make a purchase decision — a pivotal point in the buying cycle. Decision-stage content often features differentiating information, demos, trials, tools and comparison pieces, as well as content pertaining to the next steps once the purchase has been made.

Welcome to Your Relevant Outcome.

Once you understand the problem and can articulate the solution, you begin building the Relevant Outcome. A relevant outcome is equal to a customer saying "I need a ride across town and I cannot be late." Don't tell him how to build a car. Swing open your door and tell him to jump in, get him to where he needs to be, on time, and you have provided a relevant outcome. Too often we want to over-understand the problem and over-engineer the solution. Both are tantamount to failure. Solve the problem, win the customer. Solve all of their problems over time and solidify the relationship.

Most of this new philosophy is based in content. A lot of content. Marketing's role is the constant creation and modification of relevant content and continuously personalizing it for the Relevant Persona. Content is always king.

What are Relevant Outcomes?

This is when you are successful in getting the right content in front of the right persona and BOOM, that persona choose to act. Or in sales, a relevant outcome would be when you address their pain point and present a solution to solve that pain point. Marketing helps win their attention so that Sales can win the business. That is a relevant outcome.

NOTES:

"The company that operates on the words 'we've always done it that way' is writing its own epitaph"

Ned Fasullo

Content Channels

I often hear fellow marketers discussing their "social media strategy" or their " LinkedIn strategy" or their "radio strategy" and it really confuses me. I think a big problem with marketing in general is that marketers and business owners are confused as to what these platforms represent.

So let's assume that you are following the impetus of this book so far and you've bought into the fact that the foundation of good marketing is the message, i.e. content. Now let's further assume that you buy in to the ideas around the types and variety of content that should be created. If those assumptions are correct, then this next part should fall in to place.

Facebook, LinkedIn, Twitter, Email, TV, Radio, Billboards, Print, Mailers, etc are all just CHANNELS through which you deliver your message but deliver it to the proper persona within your target customer profile. The message is designed to accomodate the requirements and/or nuances of each particular channel but the message remains intact.

Example: ABC, Co. sells tractors. They want to create a marketing program around selling a particular type of tractor, the ABC-1000. The ABC-1000 can be used in a residential setting or a commercial setting and can be sold to both private and public sector. ABC, Co.'s marketing team has created a baseline marketing message about the ABC-1000. What to they do next? Blast that to Facebook? Email it to their customers? Buy a billboard? Sadly that's what most marketing departments tend to do and most company leaders frown upon because when little to no results are returned, it's deemed a waste of money, thus the step-child that is marketing.

One way to attack this is to define a simple process to assure proper execution of your message, to the right people, on the right channels.

Step 1: The Baseline Message (BM). Create the baseline message or 'offer' or whatever you want to call it. Try to keep the BM to just text and no more than one full page. Narrative or bullets, it doesn't matter just get it down on paper.

Step 2: Target Customer Profile (TCP). What customer/prospect segment does the BM play to? As in what type of company, what industry, what geography, etc.

Step 3: Content Personas (CP). Within the TCPs, what CPs are being targeted with the message? Who are they? What are their pains? What are their buying triggers?

Step 4: Define Your Channels. Based on steps 1 through 3, you now can target which channels to use to deploy your message to yield the best results.

So here's where some of the biggest changes are occurring in modern Marketing. Marketing professionals must come to accept the difference between perception and reality. Perception is that Social Media is marketing. Reality is that Social Media is just a set of channels to deliver timely, relevant content in multiple formats, sometimes for multiple initiatives. Perception is that Email blasts are marketing. Reality is that Email blasts are another channel for distributing content.

You don't need a Twitter strategy. It's a system for posting 140 character content pieces. A strategy around this is ridiculous! It's like building a strategy for going to the bathroom. You don't have to - you just go! Many may argue that I am way off base here, but I do not believe I am.

Some businesses may use all of these or just some, again its different for every business based on what they sell, but all businesses must understand the difference between an outlet for distribution of content and a go-to-market strategy.

NOTES:

"Your business' data analytics is the DNA of your company. You cannot deny the DNA for what it is or isn't. You can argue against it, but like all living things, we will always come back to what we are. You can mutate it to suit your own beliefs and desires, but with mutation comes an uncertain outcome 100% of the time. You must accept what it is and what it is telling you and play to the strengths of it to be successful"

Ned Fasullo

Your Marketing Team

So how do you build a team to handle Markenomics concepts? Well again that's a tough one, but here are some basics for what you need and what you don't need in a Marketing Department. These are by no means conclusive as far as the list goes.

What you don't need anymore:

- *A Social Media Person.* Social Media is not a job description in a B2B environment. Social Media is a channel for content. Notice I called it a 'channel'? Social Media is not a discipline, it's a distribution system for content. Besides why hire someone to post content blurbs to Social Media, when most 6th graders can do it for free? It's a title that fit at the dawn of the Social Media age years ago but is no longer relevant for B2B. Let your automation platform handle the heavy lifting of distributing the content and providing tracking on your inbound replies.

- *An Events Coordinator.* Again I struggle with these types of positions in B2B organizations but continue to see them being hired all the time. This position is a waste of time, money and resources. Let the front desk receptionist or office manager at your office handle booking rooms and food for events.

- *A PR Coordinator.* Unless you are in politics or are representing a pop star, there is little to no need for a Public Relations Coordinator. If you are wanting a way to get information to local, regional or national press.

- *A Marketing Director.* Unless you have a seat at the leadership table, this is a fluff title. Marketing Directors are mostly the folks tasked with low-level duties and are not concentrated in strategies around inbound, outbound, conversion and customer lifetime values.

What you need now (depending on the size of your organziation):

- *A Chief Marketing Officer / VP of Marketing.* This cannot be just a fluff title. This is now a key position on any executive leadership team. This role requires someone with both experience and leadership qualities. Someone with a strategic and analytics driven methodology for achieving success, and above all, someone who can inspire his/her team in both marketing and sales.

- *A Customer Evangelist / Experience Specialist.* This new position is defined almost exactly as the name says. Taking a person and making them a true evangelist for your products and services, predominantly through face-to-face and Word of Mouth Marketing (WOMM). They become a voice that is constantly trumpeting the amazingness that is your organization, meeting with the customers on a very regular basis and assuring that the customer never forgets how great it is to be your customer.

- *A Product Marketing Specialist.* This position maintains both intellectual and tactical ownership of one or more products and services. This person is tasked with managing the continuous lifecycle of certain products and services up to an including ongoing internal and external training for the life of the product.

- *A Product Development Manager.* This position sits one level higher than the Product Marketing Specialist, and is generally the lead for ALL product development managing a team for developing products and services from concept to reality. This process is managed through a combination of me imperacle data from marketing and competitive intelligence, sales pipeline, etc.

- *A Marketing Automation Specialist.* This position is one that owns the system through which inbound/outbound marketing is implemented. This is your HubSpot, Marketo, etc. champion who manages and grows the platform to continue to meet the needs of the organization.

- *Inbound Marketing Specialist.* This position should answer to the CMO and in charge of parsing the inbound leads from the marketing automation platform into the CRM for assignment to the Lead Nurturing Specialist. In smaller companies these two positions can and should be combined as one.

- *Lead Nurturing Specialist.* This position if stand-alone, takes the inbound leads from the CRM and begins campaigns to nurture the leads for a call-to-action (CTA). Generally this is done through email campaigns that introduce content that the recipient has viewed at some point, to attempt to capture the interest for a CTA. Once the CTA is confirmed, this position assures that it is assigned to a sales person with a limited window for action.

- *Content / Creative / Writing Specialist.* In Markenomics, content is king. There is no job more important in the 3.0 Marketing Department than the continuous creation of relevant types of content that are managed and deployed from your marketing automation system. When content production stops, inbound marketing interest goes cold, search engines and indexes begin ignoring you and soon you are fighting to stay ranked in the top 10 pages of any search engine. Content writing / creation MUST be constantly brought to life and managed with A/B tests to assure that the message is resonating with the intended recipients.

- *Data Analytics Specialist.* This position though last could be one of the most critical. In some organizations, this role may actually be under the CTO or CFO or Operations depending on the size of the company and the maturity level of the market it serves. Essentially this role manages and continuously customizes whatever data storage systems are in place to allow for high level to very granular dissection of customer and financial data. This requires constant monitoring and massaging of the platform, writing code and API's for connecting to your marketing platforms and CRM and more. This is fast becoming one of the most common and most valuable positions in organizations.

- *Marketing Intelligence Analyst.* This position deals with the monitoring and gathering of business, competitive and product intelligence. This data is mixed with your existing and inbound analytics to form the foundations of your content and messaging strategies, go-to-market products and sales training.

Naturally I'm not saying you need all of these roles to be successful. Let's say you are a small business that is generating between $2 million and $5 million in annual revenue. Your budgets don't allow for a very large marketing team, possibly only one individual. When you look at bringing that person in, challenge yourself to find one who understands how to accomplish these types of activities in their daily work-life in order to get you the biggest bang for your buck.

Also depending on what you sell, and who you sell it to, some of these roles may be irrelevant or can be combined. Remember this is a guideline, not a rule.

Want to see the Markenomics Org Chart? Go to:

http://www.sbobm.com/markenomicsorgchart

NOTES:

"If Marketing is the excution of action based on the data at hand, then sales is the execution of action based on the acceptance of the marketing effort. There can be no in between."

Ned Fasullo

Target Company Profile

This is one area where I am drifting away from the currently accepted industry standard definition of a term. The industry sees the term Target Company Profile (TCP) as being the individual, or person, you are selling to. I disagree. I think your TCP is the company or organization and the Content Persona (CP) is the individual. By segregating your thinking in this manner, you can create a better foundation.

A company profile is a set of attributes relating to a target population, and in business, a target group of companies. These characteristics typically include demographic factors such as income, geographic factors such as region, and psychographic factors such as values.

A typical TCP will cover the following information on a potential customer/prospect:

   --> Company Type
   --> Company Industry Sector
   --> Company Regulatory Classification
   --> Company Revenue
   --> Company Current Spend on Your Product/Service
   --> Company Headcount
   --> Company Locations
   --> Company's Current Competition

This provides a very quick way for a marketing team to determine the path to engagement and conversion, and a sales team the intel needed to get competitive at the negotiating table. There are other types of accepted profiling definitions such as:

A consumer profile is a way of describing a consumer categorically so that they can be grouped for marketing and advertising purposes.

A persona profile is a way to create a portrait of your customers to help you make design decisions concerning your service.

Your customers are broken down into groups of customers sharing similar goals and characteristics and each group is given a name, and a description. Markenomics works from the stand-point of a data-driven approach. The data is what makes up the puzzle that you can assemble to get a picture into, and a view into the potential future, of what your customers/prospects buy or will buy.

Here are a few points to get you started called *"The Five Big Questions"* (O'Brion, 2013).

Who are your people?
Who are your ideal customers? Who do you serve the best? With whom do you make the most profit? Who do you enjoy working with?

What are they looking for?
What are their points of pain? What do they wish they could improve? How do they evaluate their options? What are their rational needs and what are their emotional needs?

What is your outcome?
What is the benefit you're committed to delivering for your customer? How will you make their life better or their business stronger?

How are you different/specialized?
How are you truly different from your competitors? What's something you do that they can't copy? What is your specialty? How do you narrow your focus?

What is your because?
Why should they believe you can deliver your outcome better than your competition? What language will they use when they refer to someone else, i.e. "You have to use them because..."?

NOTES:

"Your brand is defined by what people are saying about you, not what you are saying about yourself."

Ned Fasullo

Lead Generation & Lead Scoring

Okay so I'm just going to throw this out there. If your company's sales team/sales people are saying "they need more leads" I would fire them. Like all of them, immediately. We live right now in a time when information is accessible with the click of a button - literally. Saying you need assistance in finding leads is crazy. But to be fair, let's take a step back and define what a 'lead' is as well as an opportunity stage process.

Typically and as generically as possible, a lead should be defined as 'a prospect/customer that fits into a general definition of your target company profile'. Notice I said prospect or customer. That's because existing paying customers can be leads for new opportunities when your company sells more than one product/service. So with that definition, let's take a look at a typical opportunity stage process terminology that will be familiar to most sales people.

Suspect. This is a company/customer that you have identified but have not yet classified within your TCP.

Lead. This is a company/customer that you have qualified within your TCP.

Prospect. This is a TCP that you have begun to market content to in an effort to engage.

MQL (Marketing Qualified Lead). This is a TCP that has engaged with your marketing efforts and is being tracked as such.

SQL (Sales Qualified Lead). This is a TCP that has moved past engagement and is meeting with sales personnel who's job it is to convert them into a customer/sale.

Suspects and Leads can be found in a plethora of places all around you. Books of Lists, LinkedIn contacts, Facebook Friends, Twitter followers, current customers, businesses that are in your geographic areas/boundaries, association lists, chamber of commerce lists, industry periodicals and so on, and so forth.

Once you have found your stack of Suspects/Leads, what's the best way to organize them? Well in my opinion the best way, and a way that lines up with current trends in marketing automation technology is called Lead Scoring.

Lead scoring is an innovative way for sales and marketing to 'speak the same language' when it comes to prospective customers. Lead Scoring is a combination of the target's demographics (business and personal) and how and when they have interacted with your content. This collective effort of bridging who they are with what they look at, creates an easy way to rate them all and to know when is the best or most opportune moment to make contact. Timing is everything in life, and Lead Scoring allows marketers the ability to provide solid prospect data to sales teams in the most timely fashion.

Here is an example of a Lead Scoring matrix I currently use in my duties as CMO for Global Data Systems. It's a simple enough system that rates the target based on how and what they interacted with, as well as parameters for the data we already have on them (i.e. demographics).

This allows my team to provide better data that closes the sales cycle a lot earlier with better results. It also tells us who's not ready to be sold, but needs a little nurturing to nudge them forward.

Actual Scoring Parameters. A great method for your scoring parameters for this type of grid is as follows:

Score of 0 to 33 = Connect. This means that you need to establish a more meaningful connection to the target to get their scores up before engaging or trying to convert. Targets scoring in this bracket are generally not ready to do anything and just browsing.

Score of 34 to 66 = Engage. These targets are genuinely connected to you and are repeat visitors, etc. Now is the time to engage and 'nurture' these targets with more content, but not just any content. Using your personas and matching them to the targets allows you to customize and tailor the content that is of interest to these targets and that presents solutions to their challenges in the roles they play in their companies.

Score of 67 to 100 = Convert. These targets are generally ready to meet, are actively pursuing purchases, and have necessary budgets allocated. They are consuming very precise content from you on a repeated basis, filling out forms in their areas of interest, attending events regularly and are inclined to a constant, open dialogue with experts in your company.

Remember that there is no real standard Lead Scoring System because each and every business marketing this way may be slightly different than the last. It's important to identify a system based around the previously mentioned *The Five Big Questions* and how you do business.

Want to see the Markenomics Lead Scoring Chart? Go to:

http://www.sbobm.com/leadscoring

NOTES:

"One man who does the right thing each day to succeed is worth more than one thousand men who simply show up."

Ned Fasullo

Marketing Intelligence

Intelligence by definition is the collection of information of strategic value. As defined here, intelligence is the primary process for understanding three major areas:

Business intelligence. This is all about you. This is not the raw analytics mind you, but the reporting generated by the raw data. This is also your human capital, your talent, what makes your company 'your company'. Lastly this is also your market research. What does the national and global market have to say about your industry sector and customers with in it? Examples are:

    Customers by segment
    Customers by geography
    Customers by social segment
    Customers by product/service
    Customer Lifetime Values (CLV)
    Products/Services by segment
    Products/Services lifecycles
    Revenue by customer
    Revenue by area
    Revenue by Products/Services

Competitive intelligence. This is what every company should have on their plate each quarter. They should know at a very high level at least what their top 10 competitors are up to. How are they pricing similar solutions? What new offerings are they releasing? Are they hiring? Who are they hiring? Have they received awards recently? Have they grown revenue significantly? All of these and more are questions that should be monitored as a part of competitive intelligence that can come in to play when you are in a battle with them for a new client.

To create a Complete Competitive Intelligence process, focus on Markets, Products, Industries, Vendors, Customers, by Competitor. Building a simple competitive grid that shows this information by Competitor is a great start, then focus on more granular grids for certain products/services, customer segments, etc.

Product intelligence. This is a two-fold issue. Internally your sales, operations and service teams must be well versed in the pieces and parts that make up your company's products/services. If they cannot speak to them, there is little hope you can interest a potential client to want them. The second piece to this is what the market place bears with products/services similar to yours. How is it priced? Is it seasonal? Does it sell to all verticals or just some? Being well versed in this both internally and externally breeds success and a much more mature operational culture.

Customer Intelligence. This last one cannot be emphasized enough. Understanding your customer's struggles, successes, industry issues, etc. makes you more than someone selling something to them. It makes you a more invested part of their strategy to be successful. It makes you look like you arer spending the time to listen, learn and understand.

So where do you go to look for this information? There are many, many outlets for this information all over the internet.

>**News sites** - subscribe to your local daily news blasts.

>**Financial sites** - if you sell to publicly traded companies this is an easily accessible way to get the info you need.

>**LinkedIn** - I always recommend getting the premium account on LinkedIn so you can take advantage of the InMail feature.

Social Media - easy to learn more about people and companies on Facebook and Twitter.

Statista - When you're looking for statistical information, research dossiers and comparisons, you can't beat this site.

SideKick Browser App - shows you an instant snapshot of the company's website you are on with headcount, revenue and more.

NOTES:

"If you can admit the problem, then there isn't an excuse for doing it. The only excuse is why you keep doing it, when you know it's wrong and bears no fruit."

Ned Fasullo

K.A.R.E. Customers

In the last two years or so, I discovered an amazing system for creating a planning framework around a company's existing customer base. Using a system called K.A.R.E. I am able to categorize customers into different predictive groups to assist sales teams and leadership with financial data all based on the K.A.R.E. customer's current CLV (customer lifetime value). First off what does it mean?

K. (Keep)
A. (Attain)
R. (Release)
E. (Expand)

The customer's ranked as **Keep (K)** are generally customers that pay for a set of services where there is no need or desire to expand what they have at anytime. They are happy with services and can be counted on to pay whatever they are paying, without much change.

The customer's ranked as **Attain (A)** are non-customers or prospects that your company has a desire to market to and acquire as paying customers.

The customer's ranked as **Release (R)** are customers that based on lack of consistent revenues, and/or customers that are 'difficult' or 'trouble', or generally showing declines in margin.

The customer's ranked as **Expand (E)** are the customers that are currently consuming your higest margin offerings and are prime for adopting more of your products/services. They are your key customer types, usually the ones you right references and white papers on and showcase your relationship with them.

So how do you build this type of list? Essentially I built a spreadsheet, dividing it by year between one time revenue and recurring revenue. I can then extrapolate this data into charts that can show the past 3-5 years of data to help predict the next 2-3 years of opportunities.

To be very clear, this system and method is something taught by the Sandler Sales Institute when they train sales people. One major change I made was to the R. The Sandler System makes the R stand for Recapture. In their system the R's are meant for accounts that have fallen dormant in your lists.

I changed my R to stand for Release. The reason was simple. Too many companies hold on to customers that are essentially 'bad' for business. By this I mean that the customers either don't generate enough margin on what they purchase, are a part of an industry segment no longer served, consume too much of your internal resources, etc.

Being able to align your organization across all of its departments internally working to generate revenue with the highest margins is very difficult. Knowing what types of customers to market to and what customers are not a fit for your company, no matter what they want to buy or how big they are is even more difficult.

I firmly believe that one of the pillars of operational maturity is being able to say 'no'. As for the K.A.R.E. system I provide multiple examples of how to design a template in my Marknomics training class. You should check that out. :)

NOTES:

"Stop saying 'it can't be done' and start asking 'should it be done'. That is the key."

Ned Fasullo

Product Development

In most companies, you either resell someone's stuff, make your own stuff, or a mixture of both. Traditionally, and again depending on the company, Product Development is put squarely in the purview of Operations or Technical, or some type of engineering resources/personnel. Now depending on who's reading this, I realize I am generalizing at 100,000 feet, but bear with me for a moment.

Effectively though, companies exist because they have something consumers want to buy. So again, you, the company, must 'develop' your offering so its 'marketable'. So ask yourself...If you have to make something 'marketable' to sell it, why shouldn't your marketing team be over this? Think about that for just a second. Product Development in a vacuum is doomed to fail. Development of products and services must be a true team effort with your marketing team managing the process.

I've been lucky to have been involved with several companies that were, and are, still cutting edge. And with those companies I was lucky to be invited and participate with Product Development initiatives and how that related to the actions of marketing. That experience taught me a great deal about why those in charge of making things 'marketable' should always be involved in the development of the product or service.

The following is a process design of a Markenomics based approach to Product Development that I created and currently implement in my CMO role at Global Data Systems. This is a very high overview but you get the picture. I believed after creating this and studying it that it presented a fairly common sense approach to Product Development.

In the immortal words of James Brown 'let's break it down'.

Identify the Need: In any Product Development environment, something is developed because of a perceived need or an existing need. What's important about this, and what a lot of firms miss, deals with the word 'repeatable'. In other words, are we developing something that has potential to be replicated in our organization so that all of our people can sell it to a whole bunch of other people, or are we developing a single, stand-alone solution to suit the very precise needs of a small group of our customers, or even just one customer?

A lot of organizations, especially in the technology and telecommunications services sector, create highly customized solutions that cannot be easily replicated, thus producing strain on all facets of the organization from sales, to operations to service. This is the unicorn effect. The strain comes because when you are building a unicorn, it's usually so unique that you essentially rebuild it from scratch to take to the next customer, if there even is a next customer.

Want to see the Markenomics Product Development Process chart? Go to:

http://www.sbobm.com/markenomicspd

One-off's are very expensive so if you are having to produce these solutions, make sure you have a lot of margin in the deal to justify the time and expense. Isn't the idea to make your products and services easy to replicate to put into the buyer's hands?

Needs come from various avenues. Customers come to you asking for something you don't do. Or your own teams see a niche area in your markets and come up with an idea. Literally from anywhere these things fly in. Knowing how to take them through this process is the key.

Market Research: Let's face it. This is where the vacuum starts. Product Development with no market research is doomed to fail. DOOMED. When I approach this part of the process I keep it as simple as possible, mainly because I've identified three areas that make or break the decision on moving forward.

> • **Verticals.** Whatever your widget/service is needing to be, somewhere, someone has already done it and either succeeded or failed. Bottom line. Unless you're unveiling teleportation of matter, traveling successfully through a wormhole, or turning loaves into fishes, it's been done. Look online for examples that are close to what you are wanting to produce and understand how it applies to vertical market sectors. Or if what you're doing is specific to a vertical, even better. I guarantee that someone is already doing it in some form or fashion. Google it. You can build a wealth of information with just a few keystrokes.
>
> • **Competition.** As I just said, someone is doing it. Who are they? How do they position it? How do they charge for it? These are just a few of the questions that you can address.

If none of your known competitors are doing it there are two answers as to why: a) they tried and failed or b) they have not identified it as a need. In either scenario you can learn from this and have a better informed process.

- **Cost Models.** While it's true that you want to always be competitively priced, it should not be at the expense of margin and your bottom line. When addressing this section, your financial and operations teams must be in sync so that you address the costs of production, man hours of design, marketing and sales training to bring it to the street. If you come out of the Cost Modeling phase and your widget is just like everyone else's yet you have to charge twice what they are, something is wrong. Always make sure that it fits with your current financial models. Not that you can't sell it at a higher price, but should you when others will beat you on price. Then again, if you sell on value proposition and not price, then that doesn't matter either. Selling value is where you should be, not price. You sell iPhones on price, not value. You sell value around the experience of using your product/service and the ROI it brings. Value is always more expensive.

Potential Product/Service: Now that you've made it this far you are forming up your framing work for how to get this new widget built. Now comes the tough question. With everything you've discovered previous to this point, do you Build It or Buy It. Depending on your widget/service there are pro's and con's either way. If you are a publication and you are creating a new edition to your roster, you will most likely Build It because that's what you do. Maybe in an extreme case you've identified a competitor doing it well already, so then you Buy It and integrate it into your portfolio. What if you're a technology company selling Cloud Services?

More than likely due to cost, Build It is out of the question because of the massive investment so you Buy It from a proven source and resell it. Or maybe you're taking several things and combining them into one solution that you wrap your name on? Then you Build It. At any rate, this can and will wrap back into your Cost Modeling scenarios when you are pricing out the final widget/service:

- **Build It:** You've got the opportunity to bring something unique to the marketplace (i.e. unicorns), or you already build all of your offerings that are easily replicatable so you create. This can involve developing intellectual property, etc. that adds more value to your company.

- **Buy It:** Economies of scale are available due to so many large providers creating what you need, so you consume it at a wholesale level to resell to your clients at margin. Sometimes companies can grow more rapidly by having a large provider behind them and concentrating on the selling of the widget/service.

Implementation: The final phases prior to marketing and sales training is the implementation of creating this new thing. Having a process in place that includes design, build, technical testing, customer testing, beta rollout and full scale market launch is imperative. This phase can easily become a cart-before-the-horse scenario for a lot of companies rushing to get something out the door because a client will die without it. They will only die when you deliver a sub-standard offering so take the time and do it right so they want to buy more.

Here's the bottom line. You want it to run great, make sure you have top engineers working on the insides. If you want people to want to buy the damn thing, make sure you have top marketing minds working on the outside. Then you have a winning combination.

NOTES:

"Fore-warned, is fore-armed...and eight armed is an octopus"

Irwin Fletcher

Sales Enablement

Sales and marketing, oil and water. I've seen organizations where sales and marketing are completely gelled together and organizations where one does not know or understand what the other does. The fact is that both departments operate much differently from one another but they should be in lock step otherwise things will get as hairy as a European man on South Miami Beach really quick.

One of the ways that Marketing can work closely with Sales and actually provide a valuable resource is through a Sales Enablement program. What is that you ask?

A typical Sales Enablement Program is a combination of business intelligence, product intelligence, and lead generation that is positioned on a regular weekly basis to the sales teams. Setting up a system for getting information to the sales teams can be done in multiple ways. One of my personal favorites is through an online portal like SharePoint or something similar. Office 365 makes using SharePoint very affordable. Status meetings, sending via emails, using a CRM, are all acceptable ways of performing this task as well.

Basically you want to be integral to their daily efforts of their own prospecting. Get engaged with the processes your company has with regards to product training so that you can provide better intelligence on competitive products, create comparison battlecards, etc. Get engaged with local news feeds to be on top of news and info that could influence your ability to secure business and stay ahead of the pack. Work with sales reps individually and understand what their strengths and weaknesses are and provide lead generation activities based on that to maximize the effort.

All in all there are many ways to integrate Marketing into the Sales Process and allow Markeing to provide valuable Sales Enablement tools to get more done. In fact I could write a whole other book on just this topic. Hmmmmmm. Now there's an idea!

NOTES:

"I am a son of Earth and starry Heaven. I am thirsty, please give me something to drink from the fountain of memory."

Leonardo DaVinci

Marketing & Data Science

Data Science is a relatively new terminology when discussing the practice of B2B marketing. Largely used with B2C marketing strategies to break down the demographics of the consumers, Data Science marketers are now driving this action to position content engagement with the right demographic personas within business targets.

Data Science is very simply the ability to collect, analyze and report on the data your organization collects every second of every day from every system it uses. That's financial, CRM, operational, etc. By collecting this data and farming it, Marketers can gain a very granular understanding of the business itself, produce historical patterns to predict future results and use current data to influence future outcomes. Marketers must have reasonable access to the data sets in question and the ability, or systems necessary to sculpt the data into usable, actionable intelligence. Data Science is also known as Big Data.

Big Data is not a new phenomenon. In fact you can trace back the roots of Big Data to the actual dawn of the age of computing. Every time compute was activated, data is created and it continues to grow. You've all seen the infographics on how starting about 5 years ago, the explosion of Big Data began to accelerate at a pace that is unprecedented in the history of technology. A statistic quoted in an IDC and EMC report from earlier this year says that the digital universe is doubling every two years, and will reach 40,000 exabytes (40 trillion gigabytes) by 2020. (As an example a single exabyte of storage can contain 50,000 years' worth of DVD-quality video.)

Here are some amazing Big Data statistics*:
- 90% of the world's data has been created in the last two years.

- Big data is projected to grow into a $53.4 billion market by 2017, up from $10.2 billion last year.
- Enterprise businesses store 80% of all of the data being created.
- 70% of the digital universe—900 exabytes—is generated by users.
- More than 570 new Websites are created every minute of the day.
- By 2020, at least one-third of all data will exist in or pass through the cloud.
- The White House administration is investing $200 million into big data research projects.
- China will account for more than one-fifth of the world's data by 2020
- A 10% increase in data accessibility translates into an additional $65.7 million in net income for a typical Fortune 1000 company.
- 65% of senior execs say management decisions are increasingly based on hard analytic information.
- 51% say the lack of available talent is one of the biggest impediments to making better decisions with big data.

Source – Baseline Big Data Report, 2014.

As you can see the volume is only getting larger but the opportunity for what the data represents is also growing at the same rate. If you, as a Marketer, were able to access seamlessly all of your important data, how would that impact your decision making process, as well as the outcomes of those decisions? The answer is that there would be a significant up-tick in success because data-driven answers as decisions to existing problems are almost always accurate.

The Science, Not the Art. My core belief about Markenomics as a discipline and a profession is that its basis is analytics.

Everything that is everything is based on data. If you think your marketing team is on top of things because they are posting on social media, or blogging, or showing up at trade shows and talking to clients, that's only about 10% of the battle.

Marketing is a numbers game, plain and simple. If you have a CMO, VP of Marketing, marketing staff or single marketing person, and they do not have a handle on your analytics, they are failing. Your analytics are the DNA of your company. It defines what you are, where you have been, where you are, and where you are going, even before you

This is true because as human beings we operate mostly out of habit and desire, rather than logic and numbers. The logic and numbers are inarguable and you have little to zero chance of winning when you go against them (some extreme cases could be cited otherwise but those are few and extreme).

For this reasoning I have created the graphic below. This is a high level view of my belief in this statement, and there are a ton of details and sub-concepts layered that we will expand upon later, but for now, this is what you should be concentrating on.

> "Your business' data analytics is the DNA of your company. You cannot deny the DNA for what it is or isn't. You can argue against it, but like all living things, we will always come back to what we are. You can mutate it to suit your own beliefs and desires, but with mutation comes an uncertain outcome 100% of the time. You must accept what it is and what it is telling you and play to the strengths of it to be successful" Ned Fasullo

Where is Big Data Taking Us? For the past decade Big Data has been the buzz word in IT and business circles. The internet of course is the culprit, as is Facebook and all these other wonderful platforms that we load up petabytes of LOL cat photos every few minutes of every day.

The good news is that Big Data is taking us places we could have never imagined. It's unlocking the human genome to fight deadly disease in medicine, finding over 700 exoplanets per year in astronomy, giving us insight into better economic models in finance and perhaps more importantly, allowing every person on the planet to connect and interact in ways never thought possible. That is Big Data.

For the B2B organization, Big Data plays a key role in marketing, finance, sales and operations. It could be stated that Big Data is the DNA of the organization, the stuff that already knows everything and is just waiting for us to discover it, leading us down multiple paths to achieve our goals. In short, Big Data is the driving force behind some of the world's most successful B2B and B2C companies. The question really is what is your relationship with your own Big Data? How are you using that information to drive deeper and more meaningful engagements with your customers, and how are you mining that data to predict where your future customers will come from?

If your business is an SMB or a global enterprise, your very survival in a highly competitive marketplace is your ability to utilize your own data analytics to harness success.

Here are some questions to address as you begin to understand the value of your own 'big data':

- *Where is my data?*
- *Who has access to it?*
- *Does it fail over somewhere?*

- *Is it backed up?*
- *Is it secure?*
- *How can I view the data?*
- *How do I extract and manipulate the data?*
- *Is the data 'clean'?*

When you can answer these few beginning questions satisfactorily, then you are well on your way to realizing the value of the data you hold.

How Do We Make Big Data an Actionable Item? This is a question that can be more readily answered today than ever before. And the answer is 'marketing automation' and 'predictive analytics'. Marketing automation is the software like Pardot, Marketo, HubSpot, etc. that monitors and catalogs the reaction to your outward push of content. These systems are becoming very cost effective and very highly advanced in their ability to aid in predicting the inbound subjects next move, next desire, next click.

In addition to these platforms, other systems such as Oracle, Microsoft Dynamics and others allow you to see the data in a much more raw format and build reporting on the sets of data as you see fit, and even connect to your automation platforms to pass information back and forth as needed. In order to make Big Data actionable, you must have a way to view, catalog, manipulate and report on the information. Nearly impossible to accomplish without a way to access and view the data. This is where the platforms come into play. At the end of this book I have a helpful Resources section which lists most of the major marketing automation players out there today and some of their feature sets for your review. When it comes to choosing a platform that will make your Big Data actionable, I strongly suggest you choose at least three from any list, then get a formal presentation and demo of each before making your decision. This allows you to actually have some street time with each product so that you have a good understanding of what you are walking into once the purchase is made.

Why big data is not as important as good data. Markenomics is firmly in the camp of working smart, not hard. Big Data is hard. Good Data is smart. The following article from Rudi Shumpert, Senior Architect & Evangelist, Adobe Marketing Cloud, is a fantastic insight into the deception of Big Data in the Marketing field, and why Good Data is the key.

NOTES:

"It had long since come to my attention that people of accomplishment rarely sat back and let things happen to them. They went out and happened to things."

Leonardo DaVinci

Why Marketing Matters

When you look historically at most business operations, there isn't much gray area to whether or not marketing is being utilized. You have those that claim to have a marketing person or department, and those that say they do not. So what's missing? How do you write a book to explain the value of marketing to the start-ups, SMB's and mid-market firms, while showing enterprise business a totally new way of approaching the world's 1st and oldest profession. Notice I said 1st and not 2nd or 3rd? We all know what the 2nd oldest profession is. If you don't, check out the story of Adam and Eve. My idea though is that before Eve 'laid down the gauntlet' so to speak, she had to convince her target audience that her product was THE one. That's marketing.

The bottom line is that if you want to run a successful business, generate growth revenue, not just sustaining revenue, build culture, grow and retain your customers, then marketing must play a key role in your plans. But this is just a statement, not a matter of purpose. Actually you must rephrase the question and say, 'what is the purpose of marketing in my company?'. In order to answer this you need to address a few common business questions:

- *Who are we?*
- *What do we do?*
- *What is our company culture?*
- *Why do people want to work for us?*
- *Why do vendors want to work with us?*
- *Why should customers do business with us?*
- *What differentiates us in the marketplace?*
- *What makes our products/services valuable to customers?*
- *What are our company's goals over the next five years?*
- *Will marketing help us answer and/or execute on any of these questions?*

These 10 questions are the start of a marketing plan. So can your company answer these ten questions without asking a few hard questions? Or without uncovering some of your own skeletons in the closet? Most companies cannot, which means that while there is a foundation, it has cracks. Marketing is your foundation specialist. Marketing should be implemented to help shore up the cracks today and guard against them in these areas in the future.

If I am right in saying this, then you should be realizing that true marketing touches a lot more of your company than you thought. This is why marketing matters. It matters because it is, and must be accepted, as an integral part of the engine that moves your company forward. It must be accepted as a part of the culture of how you do business each and every day, touching your brand, your communications channels, your customers and your employees.

Marketing matters because without it your business cannot really expect to thrive, and certainly can expect to make bad decisions off of faulty or no data at all. You won't understand your client base, you won't understand where your efforts should be concentrated and where they should be removed. It is as critical as anything else that happens in the organization, more so because it is intimately attached to sales and the customer experience.

I've also read recent articles on news outlets about what Marketing "is". Some say it's a bridge between the target and the company while others say it's a tool to create desire, blah, blah, blah. I disagree whole-heartedly. Marketing is a business practice that is built upon economics, demographics and mathematics. Marketing is measureable. Marketing impacts the bottom line. Marketing is vital to the survival of almost every business in some way, shape or form. At the end of it all, Marketing matters.

The question is whether your organization understands how to deploy a practice around Markenomics and measure it the same way as Operations and Finance. Until you can answer that question, then it may not matter to you at all.

The True Value of Marketing. Here's the billion dollar question from most people in the C-Suite. What is the true value of Marketing to the organization? The answer is simple because Marketing done right impacts almost ALL of the organization from top down. Some of you just read that sentence and said to yourself "bull$@*# - prove it!". Well this book aims to bring the answers you seek.

As I mentioned previously, true Marketing is a business practice founded on economics, demographics and mathematics, and as such needs to have a seat at the business table. It has its platforms for measuring and monitoring its effectiveness just like operations, sales and finance. It has measureable revenue results it can provide just like operations, sales and finance. If all of this is accurate why are so many businesses struggling with the decision around Marketing?

In order for Marketing to be effective it does have to have pieces in place to support it. First is people. Second is technology. Third is a clearly defined strategy or set of strategies as a road map. Fourth is content, content, content. You must tell the story! With any of these pieces missing, the effort will be somewhat hit or miss no matter how good you are.

Marketing's value to the C-Suite and/or leadership team seems to be a topic of much debate the last 3 years or so. Conveying Marketing's value here has always been challenging. It is easy for leadership to see the marketing dollars spent, but generally difficult for them to measure what impact (if any) there is. Sales teams are always credited with the revenue generation, but one of the main principles of Markenomics, is to re-envision the Marketing team as a revenue center. In order for this to happen, Marketing must be able to speak to key metrics and KPI's to show leadership the direct revenue related results of their actions. These KPI's and metrics will vary depending on the organization and what they sell and who they sell it to, but generally speaking you are looking for inbound conversion rates as a good start.

Another piece to this puzzle is that you are providing KPI and metric data on Marketing tactics to a group that is largely ignorant of these terms and figures. When presenting these facts, make sure you are providing them in a way that non-marketing professionals can understand and appreciate them.

Ultimately, if Marketing does not yet have a seat at the leadership table for the organization, then there is a short-coming here that is very tough to overcome. Smart organizations know that Marketing has a large stake in the success of the company as a whole, not just with the Sales teams. Change must start here.

NOTES:

"There are three classes of people: those who see, those who see when they are shown, those who do not see."

Leonardo DaVinci

The 12 Impact Points of Marketing

I've come up with 12 impact points for marketing in most organizations. This is by no means an absolute and could be different depending on the type and size of the organization as well as by what they sell. For general purposes however I have put own the 12 impact points that I believe I as a CMO am helping to impact and influence as a part of my marketing cycle.

1) Customer Experience. The ultimate goal of a B2B organization must be a satisfactory customer experience. The customer experience is the overall view the customer has of doing business with your organization, and more importantly, how they 'feel' about your organization. Why the feeling is important is because they aren't always just popping up to buy something. As a B2B you train them, support them, and hopefully help them plan for the future. If your organization has a consistency in what the customer feels when interacting with you, then you are laying the foundation for the long term relationship that is so coveted by B2Bs.

There are many, many ways that B2B organizations perform to create, enhance and maintain their customer experience. Things like customer-centric events, entertaining, tail-gating during football season, providing annual reviews, sending holiday cards are only a portion of what you can do to create a happy customer experience. Organizations that concentrate on this aspect of marketing generally receive consistently favorable reviews from their customers as opposed to the ones that are only engaged when a purchase is needed. Statistically one of the most solid and consistent ways to create and maintain a positive customer experience is a customer newsletter.

2) Operational Execution. When Marketing is clicking on all cylinders, it, like Santa, knows when you've been bad or good. Marketing is a primary touch point for current clients as well as prospects. When sales executes and brings home the contract, next up in the batter's box is the Operations team for implementation. Marketing gains a unique perspective on the beginnings of the Customer Relationship and what the future holds for the CLV of said client. Marketing can become a strategic partner to Operations or its worst cheerleader for the things it is hosing up for the clients. My suggestion is always that Marketing remains the Switzerland in the equation between Sales, the Customer and Operations so that a smooth onboarding, implementation and launch are all but a guarantee for the Customer. Squabbling between departments at the expense of the Customer is unacceptable-bar none.

3) Business Intelligence. In my humble opinion, no Marketing Department can be successful without some level of Business Intelligence activities. BI, as its referred to in the industry, is a practice of understanding your business from a vertical and industry perspective, your competition, your products and services and how they align to your vertical and industry, your customers for what they consume, when they consume it and what they spend to consume it, and finally the geographic portion of this collection of demographics and econographics - where do your dollars come from in terms of territory?

BI is critical for planning, forecasting and development. Without some portion of this, you are effectively shooting in the dark or going with your gut, neither of which provides you with hard science to back up the feeling. But BI takes time. It is a heavily time sensitive and time consuming task that is a great vehicle for your interns. Yes that's right! I am handing off what is potentially one of the most critical areas of marketing data to an inexperienced and probably business immature person/s. Why would I do this? Several reasons:

    a.) Interns are cheap labor. Create a relationship with local high schools and colleges for free interns. The younger generation is much more in tune with using the Internet to get the information that you are wanting and they can do it much faster than you.

    b) College marketing departments. Try approaching the local 4 year colleges and meeting with their marketing and advertising class Deans. Work a deal that allows them to make one of their semester projects a large chunk of your BI needs for that year.

If Marketing is truly more science than art, then BI is a critical piece of the equation for success.

4) Sales Execution. While this is probably an obvious statement, no matter how good your marketing is, if sales cannot execute, then nothing moves. Companies must realize that as Markenomics takes effect in B2B, Sales needs to take its queue from Marketing. Think of Marketing again as the CIA. Marketing has the intelligence, the products, the services and the most effective ways to penetrate and get in front of the client. Sales is the soldiers on the field. They need to take this information and apply it to their action plans. Too often in B2B organizations if there is a disconnect between Marketing and Sales, or if Marketing is relegated to the "brochure brigade", then Sales is doing its own thing, usually with little to now actionable intelligence, thus time and money is wasted. Sales is vastly important to any organization, but not at the expense of Marketing, and subsequently, Operations/Support. Remember that the effort of bringing a lead to a prospect to a paying client is only one half of the life cycle. After a paying client is on-boarded, Marketing and Operations are still working with the client for the remainder of the lifecycle.

Marketing must take the lead from a strategy and go-to-market perspective so that Sales has one main task, open the door, discuss the pain and execute. Besides at the end of the day that's the only thing that most good and great salespeople really want to do anyway.

5) Innovation. Besides the CTO, the CMO of any organization must be at the forefront of innovation. Innovation in all aspects of the company, not just the products and services to take to market. In fact, I believe that all mid-market and larger organizations should invest the time into forming an internal innovation team made up of key members of the staff and to include representatives from your top 3-5 clients. This approach allows for a larger voice to be heard internally, more people buy in thus more want to see things come to fruition. This also allows for you to gain valuable insight into your Customer's industry segments to help seed product development needs before the competition in the market even knows there is a need.

6) Product Development. While Marketing should not be in total control of this area, having it managed and driven by Marketing is a very smart move. Most would probably disagree but remember i just said "drive & manage". Having Marketing oversee the processes provide the Executive Team the ability for a top down view into the process and to protect against creating things that no one wants to buy in the first place. Here's an example of the Product Development process that I created for use at Global Data Systems. It's not fancy but it addresses all the areas that require attention. I then use the MindJet online software to create MindMaps of each product being developed that allows me to collaborate with the necessary team members, while utilizing a due date and tasking system to keep everything on track.

7) Attach Rate. For those not in the know, Attach Rate is what you get when you sell additional products/services to existing customers to increase your revenue build from each one. In other words, 'how many hooks' do you have into your customers? While this terminology may not sound on the up and up, it's widely used in the technology and telecommunications sector to describe the level of revenue depth you are gaining. The prevailing theory is that the more 'hooks' or revenue depth you can create with each customer, the stronger the financial relationship with the customer becomes, and the less likely that the customer will need another vendor when issues arise, and sometimes even protect the organization when bumps occur that sometimes cause customers to look elsewhere.

There are many reasons that organizations want to build attach rate with their customers, even those that sell products as opposed to annuity or recurring fee services. Attach Rate is at the heart of what almost all organizations want. What's the easiest path to Attach Rate? Well trained employees, strong Culture, and a great Customer Experience. Oh and quality products/services ain't too bad either.

8) Target Client Profile / Persona. In ancient warfare, the Archers were called upon for their incredible accuracy. They were used to cover their fellow soldiers on the ground because using their bow and a single arrow could strategically take out the targets that posed the most serious threats. So to, must your business call upon its Archers to wield their arrows at strategic targets. Sales people are your soldiers on the ground. Marketing is your company of Archers, their quivers full and ready to strike for the most damage possible.

9) Company Culture. Marketing's effect on company culture is the internal parallel to the customer experience. While some organizations allow their culture to come into existence organically, or naturally, others struggle with finding their internal identity. A positive company culture is a huge asset in multiple ways. Most important is that your employees are the organization's best customers. When they enjoy what they do, feel appreciated, feel like they can contribute, etc., they are highly likely to relay that positive sense of achievement through their thoughts, actions and voice when dealing with customers. Customers pick up on that almost immediately and that positive energy flows both ways.

Other organizations say that culture is up to HR, or should come from the top down (i.e. owners). I don't disagree that those departments can help set the tone and manage the benefits of the culture, marketing must be involved as well. Marketing's involvement means that a consistent tone is set across Customer Experience and Company Culture so that all parties come away with the same message, same feelings, etc. when they interact with the organization. I think at the end of the day you are only as good as your happiest client and your unhappiest employee. Culture and Experience lead the way in both of these areas.

10) Employee Development. So this one may seem like a real long shot or even down right confusing to some. What could Marketing possible influence in the realm of employee development? As it turns out quite a bit.

When you think of Markenomics think of how it touches so many parts of the organization both directly and indirectly in many ways. Let's address some of these.

11) Recruiting. This is a no-brainer. Who better to be a cheerleader for your organization to recruit new team-members than your own Marketing department? If the department is good enough to be the voice of the company outward to its clients and prospects, then it should damn well be good enough to help human resources in recruiting efforts.

12) Sales Enablement. Under Markenomics, the department will be actively involved in the development of the organization's products and services, creating the go-to-market strategy with leadership and all associated sales and technical collateral. This makes the department a perfect fit to assist the sales leadership with both initial and ongoing training to keep the teams in top form with changes and enhancements to the offerings.

NOTES:

Glossary of Marketing Acronyms

Action. Within the confines of this workbook, the term "action" means the execution and distribution of the message, i.e., social media channels, print channels, digital channels, etc.

AIDA: Attention/Awareness, Interest, Desire, Action. The four steps of the now somewhat outdated Purchase Funnel, wherein customers travel from consideration to purchase. Learn more about the new purchase consideration cycle.

AOV: Average Order Value. This is the average dollar amount spent for each customer order.

AR: Augmented Reality. An enhanced version of reality created by the use of technology to overlay digital information on an image of something being viewed through a device (as a smartphone camera).

B2B: Business-to-Business. Companies that sell to other businesses. Examples: Salesforce.com, Google.

B2C: Business-to-Consumer. Companies that sell directly to consumers. Examples: Amazon, Apple, Nike.

BANT: Budget, Authority, Need, Timeline. The four criteria sales reps use to qualify prospects. A famous tool for sales reps and sales leaders to help them determine whether their prospects have the budget, authority, need, and right timeline to buy what they sell.
- *B = Budget: Determines whether your prospect has a budget for what you're selling.*
- *A = Authority: Determines whether your prospect has the authority to make a purchasing decision.*
- *N = Need: Determines whether there's a business need for what you're selling.*
- *T = Timeline: Determines the time frame for implementation.*

BR: Bounce Rate. Website bounce rate: The percentage of

people who land on a page on your website and then leave without clicking on anything else or navigating to any other pages on your site. A high bounce rate generally leads to poor conversion rates because no one is staying on your site long enough to read your content or convert on a landing page (or for any other conversion event). Email bounce rate: The rate at which an email was unable to be delivered to a recipient's inbox. A high bounce rate generally means your lists are out-of-date or purchased, or they include many invalid email addresses. In email, not all bounces are bad, so it's important to distinguish between hard and soft bounces before taking an email address off your list. Learn about hard and soft bounces here.

CAC: Customer Acquisition Cost. This is your total Sales and Marketing cost. To calculate, follow these steps for a given time period (month, quarter, or year):
·*Add up program or advertising spend + salaries + commissions + bonuses + overhead.*
·*Divide by the number of new customers in that time period.*
·*For example, if you spend $500,000 on Sales and Marketing in a given month and added 50 customers that same month, then your CAC was $10,000 that month.*

CAN-SPAM: Controlling the Assault of Non-Solicited Pornography and Marketing. A U.S. law passed in 2003 that establishes the rules for commercial email and commercial messages, it gives recipients the right to have a business stop emailing them, and outlines the penalties incurred for those who violate the law. For example, CAN-SPAM is the reason businesses are required to have an "unsubscribe" option at the bottom of every email. Learn more of the details here.

CLV: Customer Lifetime Value (See LTV). A prediction of the net profit attributed to the entire future relationship with a customer. To calculate LTV, follow these steps for a given time period:

·Take the revenue the customer paid you in that time period.
·Subtract from that number the gross margin.
·Divide by the estimated churn rate (aka cancellation rate) for that customer.
·For example, if a customer pays you $100,000 per year where your gross margin on the revenue is 70%, and that customer type is predicted to cancel at 16% per year, then the customer's LTV is $437,500.

CMO: Chief Marketing Officer. The most coveted job in the marketing organization chart. A CMO's skill set is rooted in marketing fundamentals but expands into personnel development, quantitative analysis, and strategic thinking. Learn more about what it takes to be a CMO here.

CMS: Content Management System. A web application designed to make it easy for non-technical users to create, edit, and manage a website. Helps users with content editing and more "behind-the-scenes" work like making content searchable and indexable, automatically generating navigation elements, keeping track of users and permissions, and more.

COS: Content Optimization System. Take a CMS (Content Management System), and optimize it to deliver customers the most personalized web experience possible. Learn more about the COS here.

CPA: Cost-per-Action. An internet advertising model where the advertiser pays for each specified action someone takes, like an impression, click, form submit, or sale. You can decide if a given action is a lead or a sale. Marketers use it to figure out spending for the desired action they're are driving people toward.

CPL: Cost-per-Lead. The amount it costs for your marketing organization to acquire a lead. This factors heavily into CAC/CoCA, and is a metric marketers should keep a keen eye on.

CPM: Cost per Thousand. Abbreviated as CPM (the letter "M" in the abbreviation is the Roman numeral for one thousand). CPM is used by Internet marketers to price ad banners. Sites that sell advertising will guarantee an advertiser a certain number of impressions (number of times an ad banner is downloaded and presumably seen by visitors.), then set a rate based on that guarantee times the CPM rate. A Web site that has a CPM rate of $25 and guarantees advertisers 600,000 impressions will charge $15,000 ($25 x 600) for those advertisers' ad banner.

CR: Conversion Rate. The percentage of people who completed a desired action on a single web page, such as filling out a form. Pages with high conversion rates are performing well, while pages with low conversion rates are performing poorly.

CRM: Customer Relationship Management. A set of software programs that let companies keep track of everything they do with their existing and potential customers. At the simplest level, CRM software lets you keep track of all the contact information for these customers. But CRM systems can do lots of other things, too, like tracking email, phone calls, faxes, and deals; sending personalized emails; scheduling appointments; and logging every instance of customer service and support. Some systems also incorporate feeds from social media such as Facebook, Twitter, LinkedIn, and others. The goal is to create a system in which Sales has lots of information at their fingertips and can quickly pull up everything about a prospect or existing customer.

CRO: Conversion Rate Optimization. The process of improving your site conversion using design techniques, key optimization principles, and testing. It involves creating an experience for your website visitors that will convert them into customers. CRO is most often applied to web page or landing page optimization, but it can also be applied to social media, CTAs, and other parts of your marketing. Learn more here.

CTA: Call-to-Action. A text link, button, image, or some other type of web link that encourages a website visitor to take an action on that website, such as visiting a landing page to download a piece of content. The action you want people to take could be anything: Download an ebook, sign up for a webinar, get a coupon, attend an event, and so on. A CTA can be placed anywhere in your marketing -- on your website, in an ebook, in an email, or even at the end of a blog post. Learn more about how to make CTAs effective.

CTR: Clickthrough Rate. The percentage of your audience that advances (or clicks through) from one part of your website to the next step of your marketing campaign. As a mathematic equation, it's the total number of clicks that your page or CTA receives divided by the number of opportunities that people had to click (ex: number of pageviews, emails sent, etc).

CX: Customer Experience. Customer experience refers to the total of all experiences the customer has with the business, based on all interactions and thoughts about the business. Discipline. Within the confines of this workbook, the term "discipline" means Marketing.

DMP: Data Management Platform. This is a platform that manages types of data that can be reported on, communicated with back and forth and published outward to other systems for reporting and/or display.

DRM: Digital Rights Management. DRM is short for digital rights management, a system for protecting the copyrights of data circulated via the Internet or other digital media by enabling secure distribution and/or disabling illegal distribution of the data. OMA DRM is a Digital Rights Management standard published by the Open Mobile Alliance.

DM: Direct Mail, or Direct Message (Twitter).
· *Direct Mail: The delivery of advertising material to recipients of postal mail; also called "junk mail" by its recipients. Direct*

mail is a dubious investment for most businesses.
· **Direct Message:** A message on Twitter used to get in touch with a Twitter follower directly and in private. DMs can only be sent to your followers.

DRA: Direct Response Advertising. Promotional method in which a prospective customer is urged to respond immediately and directly to the advertiser, through the use of a 'device' provided in the advertisement. These devices (called direct response mechanisms) include a (1) coupon to cut and mail, (2) business reply card, (3) toll-free telephone number, or, on the internet, (4) hotspot to click. Most retail sale advertisements are direct response ads in one way or the other.

DSP: Demand Side Platform. A demand-side platform (DSP) is a system that allows buyers of digital advertising inventory to manage multiple ad exchange and data exchange accounts through one interface.

ECPM: Effective Cost per Thousand. Effective cost per thousand is a helpful evaluation tool that reflects the actual advertising cost per mass sales campaign. For example, if a website offers an eCPM rate of $40, and then sets the ad banner impression guarantee at 400,000 times, the eCPM would be calculated by multiplying $40 by 400 (400 units of 1,000). The advertiser's cost would be $16,000.

EPC: Earnings per Click. (EPC) A metric used to indicate the average earnings generated as a result of 100 clicks on an affiliate marketing link or ad.

GA: Google Analytics. A service by Google that generates detailed statistics about a website's traffic and traffic sources, and measures conversions and sales. Marketers use it to get to know their audience, trace their customers' paths, and make a visual assessment of how visitors interact with their pages.

HIPPO: Highest Paid Person's Opinion. HiPPO is an acronym for the "highest paid person's opinion" or the "highest paid person in the office." The acronym is used to describe the tendency for lower-paid employees to defer to higher-paid employees when a decision has to be made.

IP: Intellectual Property. IP is a work or invention that is the result of creativity, such as a manuscript or a design, to which one has rights and for which one may apply for a patent, copyright, trademark, etc.

Lead: A lead is valid once an initial click has happened on some content or messaging or advertising from us and our marketing automation system is now tracking this individual. This individual also must align with at least one of our TCPs/BPs.

K.A.R.E. (Keep, Attain, Recapture & Expand) This is an acronym for a program centered around a deep dive analysis of your top 300 clients by revenue, revenue types, business and industry demographics. The purpose of this type of program is to provide field and inside sales personnel with a granular overview of the strategic value of your top accounts.

KPI: Key Performance Indicator. A type of performance measurement companies use to evaluate an employee's or an activity's success. Marketers look at KPIs to track progress toward marketing goals, and successful marketers constantly evaluate their performance against industry standard metrics. Examples of KPIs include CAC (Customer Acquisition Cost), blog traffic sources, and homepage views. Choose KPIs that represent how your marketing and business are performing. (Learn more blogging KPIs here.)

Measurement. Within the confines of this workbook, the term "measurement" means 'the ability to report and measure on one's strategies, actions, etc.'

MoM: Month-over-Month. Changes in levels expressed with respect to the previous month. These changes are more volatile than QoQ or YoY and tend to reflect one-off events like holidays, website troubles, natural disasters, and stock market crashes. Compare the average of whatever you're measuring in Month X with Month Y to calculate the MoM change.

· To calculate percentage growth: Month X number minus Month Y number, all divided by Month X number, multiplied by 100.

MQL (Marketing Qualified Lead): A marketing qualified lead (MQL) is a lead judged more likely to become a customer compared to other leads based on lead intelligence, often informed by closed-loop analytics.

MRR: Monthly Recurring Revenue. The amount of revenue a subscription-based business receives per month. Includes MRR gained by new accounts (net new), MRR gained from upsells (net positive), MRR lost from downsells (net negative), and MRR lost from cancellations (net loss).

NPS: Net Promoter Score. A customer satisfaction metric that measures, on a scale of 0-10, the degree to which people would recommend your company to others. The NPS is derived from a simple survey designed to help you determine how loyal your customers are to your business.

· To calculate NPS, subtract the percentage of customers who would not recommend you (detractors, or 0-6) from the percent of customers who would (promoters, or 9-10).

Regularly determining your company's NPS allows you to identify ways to improve your products and services so you can increase the loyalty of your customers. Learn more about how to use NPS surveys for marketing here.

Practice. Within the confines of this workbook, the term "practice" means one of the multitude of areas within the discipline of Marketing, i.e., analytics, content, experience.

PPC: Pay-per-Click. The amount of money spent to get a digital advertisement clicked. Also an internet advertising model where advertisers pay a publisher (usually a search engine, social media site, or website owner) a certain amount of money every time their ad is clicked. For search engines, PPC ads display an advertisement when someone searches for a keyword that matches the advertiser's keyword list, which they submit to the search engine ahead of time. PPC ads are used to direct traffic to the advertiser's website, and PPC is used to assess the cost effectiveness and profitability of your paid advertising campaigns. There are two ways to pay for PPC ads:

--> *Flat rate, where the advertiser and publisher agree on a fixed amount that will be paid for each click. Typically this happens when publishers have a fixed rate for PPC in different areas on their website.*

--> *Bid-based, where the advertiser competes against other advertisers in an advertising network. In this case, each advertiser sets a maximum spend to pay for a given ad spot, so the ad will stop appearing on a given website once that amount of money is spent. It also means that the more people that click on your ad, the lower PPC you'll pay and vice versa. Learn more about getting started with PPC here.*

PV: Page View. A request to load a single web page on the internet. Marketers use them to analyze their website and to see if any change on the webpage results in more or fewer page views.

QoQ: Quarter-over-Quarter. Changes in levels expressed with respect to the previous quarter. QoQ numbers tend to be more volatile than Year-over-Year, but less volatile than Month-over-Month.

· *To calculate percentage growth: Quarter X number minus Quarter Y number, all divided by Quarter X number, multiplied by 100.*

QR Code: Quick Response Barcode. Scannable barcodes used by marketers to bridge offline and online marketing. When people see them, they can take out their smartphone and scan the QR code using a QR barcode (installable on smartphones). The information encoded by QR codes can include text, a URL, or other data.

QS: Quality Score. Quality Score is a variable used by Google, Yahoo! (called Quality Index), and Bing that can influence both the rank and cost per click (CPC) of ads. To determine the order in which ads are listed, each ad has the following formula run against it: bid * Quality Score.

RFI: Request for Information. A request for information (RFI) is a standard business process whose purpose is to collect written information about the capabilities of various suppliers. Normally it follows a format that can be used for comparative purposes.

RFP: Request for Proposal. A request for proposal (RFP) is a solicitation made often through a bidding process, by an agency or company interested in procurement of a commodity, service or valuable asset, to potential suppliers to submit business proposals.

ROI: Return On Investment. A performance measure used to evaluate the efficiency and profitability of an investment, or to compare the efficiency and profitability of multiple investments. The formula for ROI is: (Gain from Investment minus Cost of Investment), all divided by (Cost of Investment). The result is expressed as a percentage or ratio.

If ROI is negative, then that initiative is losing the company money. The calculation can vary depending on what you input for gains and costs. Today, marketers want to measure the ROI on every tactic and channel they use. Many facets of marketing have pretty straightforward ROI calculations (like PPC), but others are more difficult (like content marketing).

RoN: Run of Network. Run of Network advertising is a form of internet marketing where an online advertising campaign is applied to a wide collection of websites without the ability to choose specific sites.

RoS: Run of Site. Short for run of site, in Online Advertising ROS is a type of online ad buying campaign where the banner, image, or media ad can appear on any page within the targeted Web site.

SaaS: Software-as-a-Service. Any software that is hosted by another company, which stores your information in the cloud. Examples: HubSpot, Salesforce, IM clients, and project management applications.

Strategy. Within the confines of this workbook, the term "strategy" means 'one or more practices with actions and measureable outcomes.

SQL (Sales Qualified Lead): A Sales Qualified Lead (SQL) is a customer ready for action. These are the ones that fit your pre-determined criteria for what a hot lead looks like and you want a salesperson to make contact within 48 hours.

SEM: Search Engine Marketing. Describes acts associated with researching, submitting and positioning a Web site within search engines to achieve maximum exposure of your Web site.

SEO: Search Engine Optimization. Techniques that help your website rank higher in organic search results, making your website more visible to people who are looking for your brand, product, or service via search engines like Google, Bing, and Yahoo. There are a ton of components to improving the SEO of your site pages. Search engines look for elements including title tags, keywords, image tags, internal link structure, and inbound links -- and that's just to name a few. Search engines also look at site structure and design, visitor behavior, and other external, off-site factors to determine how highly ranked your site should be in the search engine results pages.

SLA: Service Level Agreement. For marketers, an SLA is an agreement between a company's sales and marketing teams that defines the expectations Sales has for Marketing and vice versa. The Marketing SLA defines expectations Sales has for Marketing with regards to lead quantity and lead quality, while the Sales SLA defines the expectations Marketing has for Sales on how deeply and frequently Sales will pursue each qualified lead. SLAs exist to align sales and marketing. If the two departments are managed as separate silos, the system fails. For companies to achieve growth and become leaders in their industries, it is critical that these two groups be properly integrated. Learn how to create an SLA here.

SMM: Social Media Marketing. The use of social media websites and social networks to market a company's products and services. Social media marketing provides companies with a way to reach new customers and engage with existing customers.

SMO: Social Media Optimization. The process of increasing the awareness of a product, brand or event by using a number of social media outlets and communities to generate viral publicity.

SMP: Social Media Platform. A social platform is a Web-based technology that enables the development, deployment and management of social media solutions and services. It provides the ability to create social media websites and services with complete social media network functionality.

SOV: Share of Voice. The percentage of total available ads that are included in a specific line item on a display ad proposal.

SOW: Statement of Work. A statement of work (SOW) is a formal document that captures and defines the work activities, deliverables, and timeline a vendor must execute in performance of specified work for a client. The SOW usually includes detailed requirements and pricing, with standard regulatory and governance terms and conditions.

Suspect: A suspect is anyone in our marketing automation system that is eligible to receive content and messaging.

SWOT: Strengths, Weakness, Opportunity, Threats. A tool that identifies the strengths, weaknesses, opportunities and threats of an organization. Specifically, SWOT is a basic, straightforward model that assesses what an organization can and cannot do as well as its potential opportunities and threats.

TOS: Terms of Service. Terms of service (also known as terms of use and terms and conditions, commonly abbreviated as ToS or TOS and TOU) are rules which one must agree to abide by in order to use a service. Terms of service can also be merely a disclaimer, especially regarding the use of websites.

UCD: User-centric Design. User Centred Design (UCD) is an approach that supports the entire development process with user-centred activities, in order to create applications which are easy to use and are of added value to the intended users.

UGC: User-generated Content. User-generated content (UGC) is defined as "any form of content such as blogs, wikis, discussion forums, posts, chats, tweets, podcasting, pins, digital images, video, audio files, and other forms of media that was created by users of an online system or service, often made available via".

UI: User Interface. A type of interface that allows users to control a software application or hardware device. A good user interface provides a user-friendly experience by allowing the user to interact with the software or hardware in an intuitive way. It includes a menu bar, toolbar, windows, buttons, and so on. Learn how to create a user-friendly website registration process here.

URL: Uniform Resource Locator. Also known as a web address, a URL is a specific character string that refers to a resource. It's displayed on the top of a web browser inside an "address" bar. Learn how to optimize your URLs for search here.

UV: Unique Visitor. A person who visits a website more than once within a period of time. Marketers use this term in contrast with overall site visits to track the amount of traffic on their website. If only one person visits a webpage 30 times, then that web page has one UV and 30 total site visits.

UX: User Experience. The overall experience a customer has with a particular business, from their discovery and awareness of the brand all the way through their interaction, purchase, use, and even advocacy of that brand. To deliver an excellent customer experience, you have to think like a customer, or better, think about being the customer. Learn more here.

VOD: Video on Demand. a system in which viewers choose their own filmed entertainment, by means of a PC or interactive TV system, from a wide selection.

VM: Viral Marketing. Viral Marketing is a method of product promotion that relies on getting customers to market an idea, product, or service on their own by telling their friends about it, usually by e-mail.

WOM: Word-of-Mouth. The passing of information from person to person. Technically, the term refers to oral communication, but today it refers to online communication, as well. WOM marketing is inexpensive, but it takes work and involves leveraging many components of inbound marketing like product marketing, content marketing, and social media marketing. Learn more about creating a powerful WOM marketing strategy here.

YoY: Year-over-Year. Changes in levels expressed with respect to the previous year. YoY incorporates more data than MoM or QoQ, so it gives you a better long-term view.

Professional Organizations & Associations

The following is a short, and not all inclusive, list of some of the more popular membership associations and organizations that are very popular with marketing professionals and those that are in the study of marketing. Most of these organizations and associations also offer training programs and professionally accredited certification programs for marketing professionals.

The CMO Collective
http://thecmocollective.com/

The CMO Council
http://www.cmocouncil.org/

Sales & Marketing Executives of GBR
http://smegbr.org/

Direct Marketing Association
http://thedma.org/

Mobile Marketing Association
http://www.mmaglobal.com/

Search Engine Marketing Professionals Organization
http://www.sempo.org/

Digital Analytics Association
http://www.digitalanalyticsassociation.org

Product Development & Management Association
http://www.pdma.org/

Information Technology Industry Council
http://www.itic.org/

Marketing Research Association
http://www.marketingresearch.org/

Association of International Product Marketing and Management
http://aipmm.com/

Adaptive Marketing Association
http://adaptivemarketing.in

Internet Advertising Bureau
http://www.iab.net/

Sales & Marketing Executives International
https://www.smei.org/

American Marketing Association
https://www.ama.org/

International Institute of Marketing Professionals
http://www.theiimp.org/

American Bankers Association
http://www.aba.com/

Business Marketing Association
http://www.marketing.org/

Pragmatic Marketing Association
http://www.pragmaticmarketing.com/

Direct Marketing Association
http://dmaeducation.org

Internet Marketing Association
http://imanetwork.org/

Online Marketing Certified Professional
http://omcp.org/

Professional Certifications

OMCP® (Online Marketing Certified Professional). OMCP is the industry's premier certification for online marketing professionals who have completed extensive training from qualified providers. Designed for those with more extensive online marketing experience, the OMCP demonstrates a thorough knowledge of online marketing concepts and best practices across one or more digital marketing disciplines.

OMCA® (Online Marketing Certified Associate). OMCA™ is a valuable entry-level certification for online marketing associates and entry-level practitioners. Designed for those with little online marketing experience, the OMCA demonstrates foundational knowledge of online marketing concepts and generally accepted practices across multiple digital marketing disciplines.

PCM® (Professional Certified Marketer) from the American Marketing Association (www.ama.org). Earning the PCM certification sets you apart from the competition and prepares you for new opportunities. Having met strict criteria established by the AMA, you can use the PCM credential to:
- *Prove you have mastered core marketing knowledge and principles*
- *Show your dedication to staying current in the marketing field*
- *Demonstrate your high professional standards*

CPSM® (Certified Professional Services Marketer Program) from the Society of Professional Service Marketers (http://www.smps.org/)

CIM® (Certified Internet Marketer) from the Internet Marketing Association (www.imanetwork.org/). The IMA Certified Internet Marketer (CIM) professional certification program provides participants with the foundational Internet marketing education needed to succeed in today's fast-changing online business environment.

CMMP® (Certified Marketing Management Professional) from the International Institute of Marketing Professionals (http://www.theiimp.org/). IIMP® accreditation CMMP® (Certified Marketing Management Professional) is a globally-recognized and well respected measure of professional and academic excellence in the practice of marketing. This program will recognize the perseverance, dedication and competence of successful marketing professionals all around the world. Those who earn the CMMP® demonstrate a deep, yet broad knowledge of marketing. It denotes high professional, educational and ethical standards in marketing and is valuable to those practitioners who earn it, to the clients and organizations they represent and most importantly to the marketing profession itself. The CMMP® program is designed for industry professionals and is considered to be the mark of distinction for those who demonstrate commitment to the marketing profession and to its ethical practice. The CMMP® designation is validation that a professional in the field of marketing has successfully demonstrated competency in the knowledge, skills and abilities required to practice marketing effectively in today's business arena. The CMMP® designation consists of the following four levels. A brief introduction of these four CMMP® designations is available as follows:

1. Associate CMMP®: IIMP® accredited Associate CMMP® is an introductory level international certification designed to cater for the needs of professional development of professionals who know about the marketing discipline but are not able to go into depths of its various concepts. It's a starter level certification for those professionals belonging to the disciplines other than marketing. Ideally it is meant for Account Officers, Marketing Associates, Client Service Representatives, Assistants to Marketing Officers, Territory Officers, Sales Officers and Call Center Officers etc. On the other hand this certification provides a base in marketing to non-marketing professionals like Engineers, Pharmacists, Lawyers, SME Entrepreneurs and Educationists etc.

Professionals who demonstrate their understanding of this fundamental level will be awarded with an international certification title. Detailed eligibility and entry criteria are available afterwards.

2. Manager CMMP®: IIMP® accredited Manager CMMP® is an intermediate level international certification designed for marketing professionals who are very familiar with various concepts of the discipline of marketing. As evolving in the field of marketing call for further professional development and requires to add value to their tasks and assignments. The certification is a good match for Marketing Managers, Marketing Coordinators, Marketing Communication Managers, Outlet Managers, Marketing Research Managers, Sales Managers, Distribution and Logistic Managers, Sales Engineers and IT Business Development Managers etc. The certification will enhance the capacity of marketing professionals and will empower them to better tackle the challenges of directing their teams and blush on the performances of their teams. The eligibility criteria and entry requirements are provided in the coming section.

3. Executive CMMP®: IIMP® accredited Executive CMMP® is an advanced level international certification designed especially for developing marketing professionals who have to meet the rapid and global competition around the world. By receiving the Executive CMMP®, marketers will be better equipped to face the challenges that technological innovations require, and it will enhance their diverse responsibilities and leadership in their respected organizations. The Executive CMMP® is targeted to Marketing professionals who possess quick decision making skills, an expertise of new product development rules and policies, and play a role in recruiting and training new professionals for their departments. The certification will not only add value to their credentials but also polish their foresight and analytical skills and prepare them for the global market. The certification is ideal for Marketing Executives, Product Planners, R&D Executives,

Seniors in Marketing Personnel Departments, Senior position holder in Logistics and Distribution professionals and/or professionals working in Executive positions in the Marketing Information Department etc. Please see the eligibility and other requirements in the following sections.

4. Chartered CMMP®: IIMP® accredited Chartered CMMP® is an international certifications developed for professionals in the senior most positions in the marketing departments of their organizations i.e. Chief Marketing Officer, Vice President of Marketing, Marketing Directors, Marketing Educators, Deputy Director Marketing, Regional/Country Head Marketing and Marketing Consultants etc. The professionals will be able to provide effective and efficient performance of their business operations/units. The credential will make them experts who are specialized in their field of operation. The certifications will enhance their ability to influence direct change in a variety of management structures while maintaining the vision of leadership, and it will sharpen their analytical and strategic planning skills. Further information about eligibility and entry criteria is discussed in the coming section.

PRC® (Professional Researcher Certification) from the Marketing Research Association (www.marketingresearch.org). The PRC is a powerful tool for individual researchers of all levels of work experience and education. MRA's goal is to encourage high standards within the profession to raise competency, establish an objective measure of an individual's knowledge and proficiency and to encourage continued professional development. Additionally, it is the hope of MRA that these certification standards will increase consumer understanding of research and foster premiere professional standards in the profession.

CMA® (Certified Marketing Analyst) from the American Academy of Financial Management (www.aafm.us)

Events & Conferences

Summit, The Digital Marketing Conference

- **What:** At Summit 2015, you'll learn how to find and maximize every marketing opportunity. Explore the latest tools and trends, hear from marketing innovators, and see how companies are using Adobe Marketing Cloud to give them the insights they need in mobile analytics, personalization, social media, and big data. Summit hosts more than 120 sessions, in nine tracks, on all areas of digital marketing: Marketing Analytics, Campaign Management and Email Marketing, Digital Experience Management, Digital Advertising, Personalization and Optimization, Social Marketing, Marketing Innovations, Hands-on Labs, Core Services, etc.
- **Past speakers include:** Robert Redford (actor/director/Sundance founder), Yancey Strickler (CEO and cofounder, Kickstarter), and Brad Brown (SVP Digital Retail, REI).
- **When:** March 9-13, 2015
- **Where:** Salt Lake City, UT

Social Media Marketing World

- **What:** This is a historic opportunity for you to connect face-to-face with the top social media marketing experts while breaking bread with like-minded peers from around the globe. Social Media Marketing World hosts 90+ sessions via four social media marketing tracks: Social Tactics Tracks, Social Strategy Track, Content Marketing Track, Community Management and Business-Building Track, etc.
- **Past speakers include:** Chris Brogan (co-author, The Impact Equation; CEO, Human Business Works), Michael Hyatt (author, Platform: Get Noticed in a Noisy World; former chairman and CEO, Thomas Nelson Publishers) and Jay Baer (author, Youtility; President, Convince & Convert).
- **When:** March 25-27, 2015
- **Where:** San Diego, CA

Content Marketing World
- **What:** Content Marketing World is the largest gathering of content marketing professionals in the world. Content Marketing World is the one event where you can learn and network with the best and the brightest in the content marketing industry. You will leave with all the materials you need to take a content strategy back to your team – and – to implement a content marketing plan that will grow your business and engage your audience.
- **Past speakers include:** Kevin Spacey (Oscar Award-Winning actor), Andrew Davis (author, Brandscaping: Unleashing the Power of Partnerships) and Ann Handley (co-author, Content Rules).
- **When:** September 8-11, 2015
- **Where:** Cleveland, OH

Digital Summit Phoenix
- **What:** Digital Summit Phoenix is geared toward senior digital marketers, web strategists, Internet executives and creative professionals in the digital community. The 2015 event promises a super-packed agenda with discussions and insightful case studies into topics such as content marketing strategies, social media innovation, B2B digital marketing strategies, multi-channel engagement and more. Bonus: Scottsdale, Arizona in February may be the warmest spot in the U.S.
- **When:** February 4–5
- **Where:** Scottsdale, AZ

ClickZ Live New York
- **What:** ClickZ New York is a leading search and social media marketing event in the industry for experienced marketing and advertising professionals. Formerly known as SES, this expo holds nine events worldwide; however, the fan favorite seems to be ClickZ New York. Marketing professionals, brand advertisers, agencies and business leaders converge here to learn more about the dynamic

digital landscape.
- **When:** March 30–April 1
- **Where:** New York City

ICON
- **What:** ICON (formerly InfusionsoftCon) is the ultimate event for small business success. Experience three days of big ideas, powerful strategies and actionable insights from speakers like Sally Hogshead, Rohit Bhargava and Infusionsoft CEO Clate Mask.
- **When:** March 31–April 2
- **Where:** Phoenix, AZ

NMX
- **What:** NMX (New Media Expo), formerly BlogWorld, brings together content creators from around the globe to learn about blogging, podcasting, web TV, video and business marketing. Nearly 100,000 bloggers, podcasters, web TV creators, traditional radio and TV broadcasters, producers, celebrities, media executives and social media marketers are expected to converge during this four-day conference. The 2014 event taught us the power of talking with, not at, our audience.
- **When:** April 13–16
- **Where:** Las Vegas, NV

SearchLove
- **What:** The well-known SEO agency Distilled puts on a hell-u-va conference each year in their hometown of Boston. SearchLove is a rockin' conference for client- and agency-side marketers. Here, you'll experience single-track sessions from the industry's top thought leaders, plus panel discussions and fun events in between.
- **When:** April 30–May 1
- **Where:** Boston, MA

Copyblogger Authority Rainmaker
- **What:** Hosted by Copyblogger, The Authority Rainmaker Conference is new on the scene, and worth every penny to attend. Marquee speakers like Daniel Pink, Ann Handley, Danny Sullivan, Chris Brogan and of course Copyblogger's Brian Clark will share their expertise on design, website content, traffic and content conversion opportunities.
- **When:** May 13–15
- **Where:** Denver, CO

ConFab
- **What:** The finest minds connect in the Midwest each May for this content strategy convention. At Confab Central, you'll find big-brand Chief Content Officers, social strategists, and even librarians—all on a mission to learn the best hacks for curating, managing and strategizing content campaigns. Here are our key takeaways from the 2014 event.
- **When:** May 20–22
- **Where:** Minneapolis, MN

SMX Advanced
- **What:** SMX Advanced (Search Marketing Expo) is organized by Third Door Media, the company behind the publishing powerhouses Search Engine Land and Marketing Land. Though SMX holds 10+ events worldwide, SMX Advanced is raved about for its fast-paced, Q&A-packed, frequently controversial and informative sessions. Forget the basics, this conference offers tips from the best SEO ninjas out there.
- **When:** June 2–3
- **Where:** Seattle, WA

MozCon
- **What:** MozCon offers three days of actionable sessions on SEO, social media, community building, content marketing, brand development, CRO, mobile, analytics and more. We walked away from the 2014 event with eight powerful

lessons about the convergence of content, creativity and marketing.
- **When:** July 13–15
- **Where:** Seattle, WA

Inbound
- **What:** Inbound is a gathering of marketing and sales professionals from around the world to learn the latest inbound marketing strategies. Held by HubSpot, the estimated 7,500 attendees experience sessions delivered by notable keynote speakers and the best and brightest in the marketing field. Enjoy innovative talks, educational breakouts, success stories, hands-on lessons, and lots of networking opportunities with brand marketers.
- **When:** Mid-September
- **Where:** Boston, MA

Pubcon Las Vegas
- **What:** Pubcon delivers in-depth sessions on social media, Internet marketing, search engines and digital advertising while offering an in-depth look at the future of technology by the world's top speakers. The conference features in-depth sessions, one-on-one conversations, breakout sessions, site reviews and riveting keynotes.
- **When:** October 5–9
- **Where:** Las Vegas, NV

BOLO
- **What:** BOLO (Be On The Lookout) brings together agency executives, CMOs and marketing thought leaders. Here, you'll learn how to propel your agency or business forward into the future. Two hundred fifty of the finest marketers are selected to attend this exclusive event held in the "Silicon desert."
- **When:** mid-October (TBD)
- **What:** Phoenix, AZ

PRSA International Conference
- **What:** PRSA's annual International Conference offers practical insights and networking for public relations professionals of all career levels, industries and work environments. With 3,000 public relations professionals and students in one area, the conference offers the best tips for digital PR, content marketing, social media and influencer marketing.
- **When:** November 8–10
- **Where:** Atlanta, GA

Marketing Technology Landscape

Each year, a great resource site called ChiefMarTec.com puts together an extremely comprehensive 'supergraphic' of the Marketing Technology Landscape. This is distrubted absolutely free on their website at **http://chiefmartec.com/2016/03/marketing-technology-landscape-supergraphic-2016/**

A few notes about this landscape:

1) The growth of marketing technology companies from 2015 to 2016 was an astounding **87%**!

2) The 2016 landscape represents 3,874 companies encompassing all areas of marketing technology. There are an additional **1,900 companies that did not make the landscape map this year.**

3) By comparison, 2011 had 150 companies, 2012 had 350 companies, 2014 had 1,000 companies, 2015 had 2,000 companies.

4) The lanscape supergraphic represents all areas of marketing technology but the **top 5 categories are**: a) Sales Automation, Enablement & Intelligence, b) Social Media Marketing & Monitoring, c) Display & Programmatic Advertising, d) Marketing Automation & Campaign/Lead Management, and e) Content Marketing.

5) The research shows one very clear piece of data: **There is no one platform that does it all**. In fact most businesses engaged in this level of marketing are actually utilizing more than one platform to accomplish their goals.

6) This year's landscape has clearly established that a 'technology stack' mentality is out and what is in are **6 Marketing Technology Capability Clusters**: a) Advertising & Promotion, b) Content & Experience, c) Social & Relationships, d) Commerce & Sales, e) Data and f) Management.

In Closing

My goals in writing this book were two-fold. First and most importantly, I wanted to try and share some of the knowledge I have collected over the years with others. Second was to serve as a primer for my marketing training system called Markenomics. The purpose of the Markenomics system is to educate business owners and executives on the value of funding a professional marketing program in their own companies.

I hope that I will succeed on both items and am already working on outlines for several new books that deal directly with tactical actions that a business can take to see a real impact in their revenue.

Marketing should never be something done "just because". Treat it like any other department in your business and see it as a vital part of what you must do each day to be successful across all of your departments.

I appreciate you giving this book a read and welcome any comments you may have. Just shoot me an email at nedfasullo@gmail.com. Looking forward to hearing from you soon!

658.8 FAS
Fasullo, Ned
The small book of big marketing : the

08/19/22

CPSIA information can be obtained
at www.ICGtesting.com
Printed in the USA
LVHW020151180622
721551LV00020B/1709